The Thin Smoke of the Heart

The Hugh MacLennan Poetry Series

Editors: Nathalie Cooke and Joan Harcourt
Selection Committee: Donald H. Akenson,
Philip Cercone, Eric Ormsby, Carolyn Smart,
and Tracy Ware

TITLES IN THE SERIES

The Thin Smoke
of the Heart

TIM BOWLING

McGill-Queen's University Press

Montreal & Kingston · London · Ithaca

© Tim Bowling 2000

ISBN 0-7735-1905-X

Legal deposit second quarter 2000
Bibliothèque nationale du Québec

Printed in Canada on acid-free paper

McGill-Queen's University Press acknowledges the financial support
of the Government of Canada through the Book Publishing Industry
Development Program (BPIDP) for our publishing activities.
We also acknowledge the support of the Canada Council
for the Arts for our publishing program.

Canadian Cataloguing in Publication Data

Bowling, Tim, 1964–
The thin smoke of the heart
(The Hugh MacLennan poetry series)
ISBN 0-7735-1905-X
I. Title. II. Series.
PS8553.O9044T45 2000   C811'.54   C99-901596-6
PR9199.3.B6358T45 2000

This book was typeset by Typo Litho Composition Inc.
in 9.5/13 Baskerville.

for my parents
who taught me to appreciate life

and for Dashiell
who makes sure I remember the lesson

Contents

I

The Line

Why did I come to it? Where is it drawn?
How does it lie, and what divide?
If I speak of blood, will you not admit
that selfsame pattern holds you up?
We are nothing but variations of it,
and when we see, and if we see, and how,
decides the nature of our step across,
by land or sea, by flesh or word.
This one points particular, this one
is the wet chalk of my life on the board.
I follow it here, to where division began.

Two o'clock in the morning and a tired man docks his boat.
He has taken four tides into his hands and few fish. Now
he's going home. Finger under the gill, he hefts a red
spring from the deck, and steps heavily onto the wharf.
The river is calm and smoking a low mist into a sky
so black the stars seem close enough to be the blur
of sleep in the man's eyes. He tenses his wrist and
trudges his gumboots over the planks and up the gangway
to the top of the dyke and down to the street, alone
with one streetlamp, his own footfall, and a line
of blood he doesn't know he leaves, a line the pull
of his finger in the salmon's gill began, a stream
along its scales that drips off its tail and marks
a black spine for the moonshadow he drags behind.

Half a block to his gravel drive, he lays the line,
the last spool of the gaping mouth. He doesn't take
the ache of it in his wrist for more than life,
the heaviness of muscle and water, for more than
one night following another in one summer following
another on the same black river. But his hand gaffed
the line and now the line is drawn and now it burns
and will not be erased. And someone else besides
the tom who creeps out of the grass to lap the spark
will wake and swallow its chill power to the marrow.

Gash of lipstick on the Salish girls the druggist's
wife remarked were sluts and stole, my mother's boss
who bid her sell the Indians the gaudy tones and save
the upscale glosses for her kind. Gash of trench
my father's father breast-stroked through, his own
blood for a pool, and all the opened veins of boys
that serviced the rank geometry of a continent.
Gash on the brow of the scab who cried fuck off
to men who blocked his path, and wore the vivid badge
for those who hid behind immaculate counting hands.
And gash of ink to keep the cheap gloss on the proper lips.

Why did I come to it? Where is it drawn?

How does it lie, and what divide?

But also it is the beautiful flesh of the inside of the throat
going all the way down to the cry of joy and terror,
and it is the long kiss and the juice of the black plum
and the tightrope over the precipice of memory and
the pricked fur of the fox's run. It is unwound from
the mouth of all the dead to be rulered by the born,
it is the tongue of the garter snake that smooths
the grass for the child to kneel, and the finger of wine
that indexes a song from the cowering heart, and it is,
and it is, the fever of the love of the sound of itself,
unwinding, strand in the web, vein in the wrist, star
in the constellation, the naming and the singing
of the felt and the seen. Tomcat at the mad wick,
I know your hunger, I came out of the cradle of blades
to taste what I did not know I was starving for,
all sides of all things, the fire in the soles
of the dancer and the mimic fire of the coals,
but more, to touch this world in its four tides,
and take from it the means to lay these down,
my variations and my nature, out of the gaping mouth
in my father's hand, a lifted selvage from the one design.

The Douglas Fir

Of all the steeples in our wet town, I recall
most its hundred feet of God-point and its peal
of shivering, tremulous cone, each cracked bell
on each frayed branch chiming a resonant whole
and calling us out of gravity back to the fold
of childhood, where green meets green in climb
and the faith of never looking down is all.

It stood limbless to the ten-foot mark, so we had to scale
its roughness hugging close until our cheeks chafed raw.
Its trunk was slick and barnacled as a killer whale
and seemed to move as much. Soaked, womb-tight, we saw
the half-inch growth of eighteen eighty-four
and then the inch of eighty-five and six. At its full
height, which we could never reach, grew the current hour.

The fir stood single in a vacant lot, its only peers the ground
from which it grew and the ceaseless rain which bid it grow.
The grass was infant at its knees, the sun and moon too old.
Unaware, we listened beyond Sundays for its plaintive sound
and came in flocks of awe and fearful joyousness
to hear a windstorm set it tolling for its loneliness.
We didn't know the keening-root predicts the keening-bone.

On moonless nights, all those stiff, shawled arms – the fir
was like a staircase being mounted by aged Greek widows,
fishermen's wives seeking an old solace for their drowned.
I could see them from my bed, those walkers black as crows
ascending beyond where the sap had hardened to an amber tear.
And I could hear the fir weep with them in the heavy rain.
It gave its love to everything that knew the weight of time.

Now it's gone, whose million needles gilled the fragrant air,
whose trunk belltowered our faith in every dusk and dawn, whose
absence leaves us doubting that our hands were ever there,
and there, and there, in the thousand places torn from the sky,
in the heaven where our heartbeats drummed the rough bark smooth.
But is it gone? I lift my eyes to where my future hid its hours
in the grain. My death settles easy in the first green pew.

The Paperboy

"Collecting for the Sun!" How often I cried
the phrase before I knew enough to know the kick
of irony. "Collecting for the Light that warms
the Earth!" Would that have hastened knowledge?
I can't recall a single headline of those years
I pedalled papers through the streets, but
feel them in me like a blackened spine, and
wear them on me like a stripe. With my sack
slung across my back and a smile slung across
my lips, I called out for my monthly cash
through doors where widowed older women sipped
their tea and called back anxious at my knock.
"Collecting for the Sun," I'd cry, and fidget
at the slowness of their aged walks. Smudged
with type, my open hands would take the folded
bills and carefully-counted coins, and tips,
oh yes, the widowed ladies always tipped. It
seemed I only had to be a child to justify
their favour, though they often asked me in
for the clichéd milk and cookies, and in I went,
all politeness for my sins, such as they were
at that age, was it eleven, ten? In any event,
I was as bored as you'd expect, and the clocks
on the mantels you'd also expect were ticking
and I could hear every long, slow second falling
from the thick hands that were hardly moving
up beside the photographs of the young couples
in tuxes and white dresses. Yet I must have known

at least something about time and sorrow when
each woman returned to me with a loaded plate
of peek freens and my glass of milk so full
I always had to take a sip to prevent a spill.
I must have known those silent hours weren't all,
that the eyes that stared me down across those rooms,
peering out above the shawled and trembling postures,
were human lessons that I'd never learn
from the sludge I carted daily on my back.

Out of the brayed cant of collection was I formed,
out of the cackle in bold type was I shaped,
out of the skulk of opinion was I striped,
but once I slipped between two pairs of eyes
like an uncried tear, and in my slipping,
found the only news worth bearing in this life.

Russ

He had hair bright as Christ's blood on the cross, and dared
the sharp gravel of the lower Fraser's dykes to prick
the same colour from his naked soles. He ran everywhere.
Ten years old, with the mouth of a stevedore, he was a spark
burning at the end of a long wick. Once, he threw a rock
through the stained-glass window of the United Church,
and defended himself, crying, "I saw the effin' devil up there!"
His father, a fisherman, weary from a long week's work
yanking leadline off snags and clubbing dogs in the stern,
paid off the minister without saying a word, then grabbed
his boy by the scruff of the neck and, as though holding the tor
of an ugly mob, lit his way to the woodshed. "Well-earned
this time," my father said, as cries broke the crystal calm.
"Sometimes I think he's right to tan the little bugger's hide."

But my father liked him all the same, liked the fact he turned
every beating into pride, dropped his pants to show the belt-
marks on his ass (he showed them to the minister: my father,
who preferred the Indians' Creator to any other god, laughed)
I loved him the way boys love, admired his reckless deeds
and tongue, and felt embarrassed by my fear, my lack of welts.
Once, I yelled "Chinky Chinky Chinaman!" at Mr. Lo, the groco
and for weeks could not go in his store. I don't know why.
Sometimes I don't think I know anything about the past
except it's past. I remember Russ and I chewed bubblegum,
and collected empties out of the river-mud and the tall grass
to cash in the deposits. We must have talked for hours,
but whatever we talked about, and how we talked, that's gone.

I don't know, sometimes life just seems to be a kind of perfume
fading faster and faster from the flower. Last time home, I asked
about him. Seems he's living north of the Skeena now, alone,
in a small cabin miles from anyone. Crippled by some arthritic
condition, he can't work much, keeps to himself, refuses to take
his medication. I remember the boy who dared fire in his soles,
the mad sizzling dance along the wick, the colours smashed
out of the dull sky, the curses, the cries, the bared ass. Russ,
I want the effin' explosion we were promised, the inverted blast
that makes the crystal vase around the flower whole.

Old Man Dunne

So thin, he seemed a broomstick his broad-beamed
and never-smiling wife simply let go of once she'd
reached the verandah and her end of dust. So hard,
he lashed the spring air like an ashplant cane
on a schoolboy's flesh. So old, he could have been
a splinter from a tropical Arctic rainforest.
His eyes were black and deep as a witch's stove.
How much we feared him. How much he hated us.
We swung in the plum trees, the apple, and cherry,
in all the common orchards of our street, singing
our names to each other like beads in a rosary.
He snapped in the honeysuckled breeze, he cried
"get down from there! get down!" In the vernacular
of our father's tongue, he was a christly holy terror
who gave us royal old hell. He thought we stole
the sweetness from the season long before its time,
and so, to keep his harvest safe, he picked the fruit
before it fell to earth or us, he picked it green.
On a wooden ladder dragged from his yard, he rose
into the boughs, like the caw in the beak of a crow;
we trembled in our caves of high grass, listening,
we sucked all the juice from the last plum-pits
and cursed him and his scowling wife for being mean.
The battle raged each spring and summer. Sometimes,
we even made ourselves sick by gorging on the green
before he raised his battered rungs into the air.

Old Man Dunne with his paper bags full of fruit.
The broomstick, the cane, the splinter and caw.
I haven't thought of him in twenty-odd years.
Not in a coon's age, in the vernacular
of our mother's tongue, not in donkey's,
not even once in a blue moon, no, never,
not in a month of Sundays. But now, I find
I press my longing to the highest branch
for fear of losing what I tasted once,
and there's a hot coal at the back of each eye
that would burn any child's bones to ash,
and such a terror of my need to lash
the sweetness in the air that I can almost pity
what I fear the most, the green heart in man
that rots to no purpose on a windowsill
under a pane of cracked and dusty glass.
And since pity is closer than fear to love,
I offer these orchards again to Mr. Dunne,
and hope that when my own spine reaches up
in cruel extension of my old hunger,
I'll smile toward the grasses, keeping
my cold step off the rungs.

The Rhododendron

Childhood has its own grave, and mine
is tombed by the purple rhododendron
blooming again in my mother's garden.

Tonight late bees engrave an epitaph
on the heavy flowerheads, and dusk
settles chalk-grains over their work.

The death of all life is sickly-sweet,
why not the years? There is no threat
in this black earth and this air wet

with the grief of stars. And rain,
each drop, stands straightbacked when
the bees have done, mourning the time

when a child breathed here and the grass
gave way to his light tread on the last
spring evening of a wonder so chaste

it was the only reality, the only truth.
A child has no patience for any death.
But once an adult, is it really enough,

this standing purple clutch of memory
washed round by darkness, night's sea
of hours on the gentle ebb, infinity

salting the petals? Time is a grave
that digs itself, and all we have
to do is consecrate it when we leave.

A grizzled black lab guards the portal
to the tomb. My mother's arms are full
with remembered weight; her low whistle

calls me back one more time to home.
But it is only my young ghost who comes,
a faded and gentle hour in his bones,

and pats the dog, and kneels in the rain,
and hears the woman's steady heartbeat again
clocking the desecrating step of the man.

II

In a Small Town on the West Coast

The seagulls' tapestry of fishgut and last light,
the ripe blackberries splotching the unfooted dust,
the ogres' sacks of human shadows heavy with hearts
and dragged over dykes, that low-tide-in-the-mouth taste:
rivertowns are always nostalgic for the day they've lost.

See how the current and the falling night flow together
on the same tracks, the ones walked by dogs and girls
and old men wedding their dusks in the briney air.
A garter snake twists into a question-mark on the rails.
A girl's body pauses long enough for her blood to answer.

The sun is always going home; with people, who can tell?
There's something harsh and honest in a screaming gull
that makes us wince, something lovely, direct and awful.
Perhaps the girl, hearing it, can cause the snake to fall.
Every myth begins where the ogre's sack is full.

Late August at the Mouth of the Fraser River

The wind pulls the full blackberries gently
from their stems, the way a woman
removes her earrings after a dinner-party,
sighing as her tongue forgets the wine
and her cheek her host's kiss. Nearby
in the boatless harbour, a muskrat swims
from darkness to moonlight, silk sliding
down the white flesh of a thigh, and on
the farther shore a pregnant doe steps out
of the woods to listen to the two red watches
ticking at two different speeds
between her tissue-paper ribs.

Silt from the mountains is filling the channel,
the slow current is making tails out of heads
on a coin dropped by one of Galiano's sailors,
and auburn is packing its only good suit
to go off on a journey through a million leaves.
The moment calls for us, but we're staying here
to allow the world its own sweet company, to
let the berries drop on the grass, the musk-
rat reach home, and the deer time her pause
by the water. Stay quiet a while. Listen
to the ticking womb. Be in the world
while absent from it, like the sun,
the dead, the panting fawn.

Bullhead Fishing

Only children care for these dead,
unhook with cautious glee the inward gulp
and frill of barbs attached to gills
and engorged eyes like poisoned moons
and fat grins clamped defiant
on the hard-spined garden worms.

Only children, dawn-dew spattered,
silent in the new sun, will lie
on broken, mossy floats,
their still-dozy faces hung
over the stink of tide and creosote
to play these ugly puppets
with skinny lines of catgut
heartbeat after heartbeat.

I cared once, and on my knees
twisted the dumb heads until
the hooks ripped out in blood
and I saw, amazed, the little
version of the larger kill
around some hook, a Chinese box
of hungering gut, the father
wild to eat his brood ...

and sunlight slick on the planks
and on my hands and in the fish's
smaller poisoned moons
in which I briefly lost myself
little knowing loss or self.

What so baits the day but images we chase
of what we were and cannot be again?
What most takes our hunger to the hook?

I saw my face unbroken in the river
and the worm descending to my mouth
shedding crumbs of earth, and the bullheads
lurking just behind my eyebones
and my lips, and the sun loosely on my hair.

But I can never see it as it was
before the dangled hook touched down
and suddenly made of intact bliss
this life of lovely fracture.

The Netshed (1)

Death that was, hung from the beams,
and death to come: torn and stained
from prior summers' snags and
                              kicked escapes
or virgin in their let-loose tresses,
we pushed with wonder back the fathoms,
                    apple-dry and apple-green,
so many thousands, all those seasons,
what the river ruined and what it would;
long veils that hid from us a harsher world.
Touching them, we shed a light on fact,
as though we'd spilled the oil in the corner-lamp,
and felt the crackle of the salmon's blood
still on the meshes like a woman's blush
from a vanished time, a vanished love.

So quickly down the plank we go
                    to meet our fates,
those shadows swaying from the beams,
the deaths that we must be and learn to keep,
not with fear but joy, and open-eyed, swiftly
in our need to make unknowing die, we break
                    the hours at their meshes
                                        and escape.

The Netshed (2)

Wise men could row to find a saviour here
mewling in burlap on a stack of fish crates;
certainly, it's no great skill to follow a star
up the mouth of the Fraser; all it takes
is one eye on the bank to keep a safe course.

There'd be screaming gulls not lowing cattle
gathered round, and scales instead of straw
and the wise men would bring other riches, oolichan oil
and a pickled seal's nose; they would drift in and bow
to a virgin with the hope of mankind at her breast.

And maybe the harbourmaster had turned her away
and her husband owned a gaff-hook instead of a saw
and the future would be Steveston not Galilee
and death would come on a current not a cross
and there'd be beer not blood to slake our thirst.

Nice try. The men are ignorant and drunk. The gulls
would tear the infant's flesh if not kept back. The woman
hasn't been a virgin in as many years as there are scales
plastered to the crates. And I've been to Steveston,
as fish-stinkin' a town as you can find on the coast.

Two Cigarettes, Burning

And no light else this night along the banks
at the mouth where the roots of rushes lick salt;
only these in the gloom of dripping rain:
still and close, the bloodshot eyes of a heron
fishing the pools forever without success;
then, in sudden motion, dice tossed in
Hell, flames blazing out the dots; only these.

And the weight of the thought behind them, heavy
as the great silver chain hauled link-by-link
out of the mud each year before it breaks
to rusted shackles in the high creeks.

And the void of the rain-obscured stars,
consciousness and nothing, consciousness of nothing;
impossible to conjure up the cheekbones or eyes,
the scarred hands, torn voices, impossible
to breathe that smoke again.

All night, the river shunts ash to the sea.

The lights burn down in the fingers of the men.

Meditation on a Fall Day

To be sad before the occasion of sadness –
the apogee of wisdom, or some sickness
of the spirit, leaf gone to earth in summer,
the salmon spreading its milt far at sea?

A social worker my older brother once dated
summarizing our melancholy brood, looked deep
into his onyx eyes, with sympathy, and said,
"you're all in a state of premature grief."

Elderly parents so loved, one with kidney illness
and the other worn out from nursing and worry.
Yet can love be too much love that it makes us
immortally distant from the gift of our mortality?

Autumnal now the years and skies, autumnal the heart
that walks its fawn's fear over twigs and starts
at every sound that augurs the sound of absence,
a siren to my siblings, the shrill cry of a phone.

What binds us firm must pain us to the very quick
when it has gone, love, memory, the familiar joke
told in the comforting tongue. But until gone,
wisdom must contain defiant glee while flesh is warm.

So to revel in what we cannot bear to lose, family
or the fragile earth, is mortality made wisest: the sea
is salt but clear of milt that serves no purpose, the sky
is without leaf but cannot stop the ascent of the forest.

Vow

A bald eagle in a riverside fir stares at
the uncarved faces of a thousand pumpkins
sagging into frost behind a barn of faded
planks. Hours pass. Who will blink first?
It is that sort of morning for the heart;
the living are giving the dead an honest test.

A man has walked out to be alone with the earth.
A man of his age, he equates time with grief
most days, but now he has decided to wait.
In the silence, where do his raised eyes fit?

I'm not that man, I'm not
between the fir and the rot
of the pumpkin fields, but
I'll pick up the gauntlet
of his morning nonetheless,

stand to the side of the fierce contest
and not make the eyes of the eagle shift.

Yesterday

An August cornfield, its slow dawn
finally breaking. Starlings in and
out like a spray of night. The low
smoke of a black lab insinuating
itself through the stalks. Along-
side, a river thick with salmon.
The dog is the closest thing
the scene has to what is human;
he comes to a cry from a throat,
he snaps the salmon's bright chain,
he is rampant as desire. The dog
bursts from the swollen light
and lies breathing in the dust,
mouth slack and open. He is heavy
as a blackberry bush fully ripe;
his tongue is the pink hand
of a child reaching always
towards its hunger.

I wore the day of stalks.
I snapped the riverchain
until it bled. I owned
the dog and put the cry into
his brain. My grip tightened
on his collar, and the little
hand drew in. O child, fast
breather, whisper our name
to the full sun again.

III

The Stillborn Child

All goes onward and outward, nothing collapses,
And to die is different from what any one supposed.
– Walt Whitman

Child
(April 1962)

Mother, they have taken me from the cradle of you,
and I fear the cradle of you was my only one.
Outside, the moon has already started to warm
the grassy roof of my longer home.

Father, they are giving me heavy into your arms,
and you have nowhere but the earth to lay me down.
You will lower me into a cradle rocked by stars,
into a womb of fire, a forgetfulness of hours.

Is it lucky to escape the sorrow of time,
not to tear the silence with a welcoming cry?
I remember the sound of my heart as a walking away.
When it grew faint, I followed. I don't know why.

What is happening? Where is the soothing voice
and the light behind the flesh? I thought I was
being led home by the footsteps of the world,
I thought I was on the warm path of my blood.

Now I am riding the salt swell of your tears
out where the moon puts a pale hand on the river
and feels the tide kick on its way to the sea.
Tomorrow I will rise to cast my shadow on the day.

The love of what I cannot touch must parent me.

Child
(June 1962)

It's June, the river high.
The windfall apples fall
in gouts from orchards torn
with stars. And I am gone.
My father drifts on the tide
beside the empty branches, all
his net upon the waters, dawn
as near and far as any pain.
My mother in her bedroom grieves
her flesh from her core, and still,
I am gone. If she stands in the window
for hours waiting, if he seeks me
in the heave of mesh, or if the bough
wants back its weight, I am gone.

And yet, what is the air but grass
that dews a fallen skin? And loss,
what is that but proof we lose
fragility of seconds and our form?

It's June, the river high,
the salmon heaving in my father's lap,
the absence heaving in my mother's arms.
Once, I tried briefly what I could not try
for long, and now it's my trying makes
the windfall apples seek their grave.

Father, Mother, my little future,
in this June of our first forgetting,
can you not hear, not hear on the air,
back of the scent of the windfall dying,
can you not hear the sweetness of life,
all the stillborn crying?

Mother
(June 1962)

High wind. The thud, thud, thud
of apples dropping in the yard
keeps me awake. It sounds like ...
a faint heartbeat. It could
be mine, or his. Since that night,
I can't say whose went, whose stayed:
any rhythm, the rain, a wasp-buzz
on the windowsill, someone's footsteps
down the hall, it's all the same.
Something is keeping time to our pain.
How many apples equal his little death?
When they've all dropped, or the wind
is still, will I know my heart again?
Now, it is one beat for pain, and one
beat to deny him to the ground, and one
beat more that could be the very sound
of the dark earth being born to the sun
each day. Days – I think I could be done
with them now. Apples in the wet grass
waiting to rot, a gutted jack in the sink,
a world of heartbeats and stopped hearts
wrenched from the unprotecting bough.

Father
(June 1962)

Thirty sockeye that drift, fifteen
kicking in the web, fifteen dead,
strangled as they thrashed in the mesh.
But for all that, they're the same
now, stiff and staring under the drum.
It's their open eyes that get me most,
the fact that they ought to see, I guess –
all that looking but the world is lost
to them forever. How not to think of him
staring dumb-mouthed in the bright light
when another's cold hands pulled him out
of the dark. How not to think of life,
all life, as the cruel odds of a hard swim
back to home. But how could he know his home
so soon? He never even touched the grass
before we parted it to dig his body down.
The wind's kicking up again, from the east
a bit now. It'll bring rain. Ah, it's a waste
of time all this! Might as well set. Gone
is gone, we can't bring him back. Christ,
I need a smoke, stop my hands shaking. It's
going to be a long night, and more to come.
There's nowhere to look and NOT to see.
Somebody's wiped fish-blood off on the moon.

Child, Father, Mother
(December 1962)

Too old to try again? I whisper them no,
their faces troubled in the midnight room.
They're afraid of death now I have gone,
and I can't tell them that the seasons go
no differently, the salmon-clock of June
replaced by winter's ticking rain, a whole
world of life come round that they will know
by standing still. Why not be active then?
I try to ask but they cannot hear me speak.
"O let me be something to you, but not all."
No one dreams how the hearts of the dead can ache.

I might as well get up since I can't get to sleep.
Listen to that rain! How the hell much can fall?
I'd better go down to the wharf tomorrow, check
the boat. It's time I pumped her out. And I'll
turn her over too. Haven't bothered in a week,
but it's getting colder now. That sleeping pill
sure has done the trick. A few hours, at least,
that's what she needs. Damned doctors! They'd make
you scared of your own shadow. But who says the best
thing to do is always the safest? I'm willing to take
the risk if she is. Life isn't a matter of what it costs.

His death between us. Nothing we do will ever quiet his ghost,
but maybe if we try? I'm not a young woman, but I'm not weak.
And no one knows anything more than we do about loss.
We haven't lived forty years without … I think I'll close
my eyes, no sense him worrying that I'm not getting my sleep.
Poor man. This has hurt him more than he will say. It was
hard to watch him stare and stare and never cry. Tears stop
eventually, but there's no end to what he sees. It's because
we both need to fill our sight with something besides grief
that it's time to ignore our fears and all the doctors' talk.
There's only one word now. Even the rain whispers yes.

Child
(August 1964)

If a hanged man falling through the gallows-trap
never stopped his fall, but went on booting light
and space forever while his eyes searched back
to find the earth, he too would know the straight
rope swinging like a pendulum between the worlds,
this rope I hold in place of a waterhole swing,
this frayed hand keeping time in the star-clock.

I fell from a warm sea, like everyone, but I swim
where I can't be held. This child, now, his look
of distress, his vernixed skin, and clutch-reflex:
when they cut his cord, he will fall from the womb
forever into our mother's arms and long-dusked summers
booting grassblades and the juice-drunk air. No husk
of his first form will darken our father's river.

What the wick is to the candle, what the twig
is to the apple, what the heart is to the flesh,
what the tongue is to the voice, we are to the future:
cut anyone's cord; the blood will not sever.

Child
(October 1969)

That's my little brother lying in the grass
watching the blood drip from the cock-pheasants
twisting limp-necked on the clothesline. That's
his dog smearing the buttery flesh of a ripe pear
over its jowls, snapping at wasps. It makes sense
to hang shot birds above the jaws of prowling cats
and for a silly dog to growl and bite at empty air,
but no one wants a boy to deeply study death. Yet
those are his eyes on the slow red rain. That's
his mind considering the wide gap between where
the bronzed bodies twist and the dotted line stops
in a puddle in the frosted grass, a sticky magnet
for blowflies (he notes their thick shadows clear
against the blue autumn sky as well as on the earth).
His wrist is bare. He's keeping time to a larger watch,
the one I've been setting for him all these years.

What is love but a gift to others of all we've lost?
Our parents gave him the love they couldn't give me,
so I'm giving him the unused language to speak my ghost,
the quill dipped in the pheasant's vein, the blobbed type
of the blowfly's hunger, the moon's chalking of the sea,
apples in the wind, high hourglass of blood, woodsmoke,
screel of gull, a dog's fur, the cracked mirror of frost.
That's my little brother leaning to my whisper in the grass.

Poet
(June 1998)

Last night I dreamed of salmon spawning
millionfold in the North Saskatchewan,
their red light a thick path off the sun
slowly setting. Hookjawed sockeye were dying
far from home, in a jade river that runs
north, opposite of the truth their fighting
instinct knows. At the sight of such loss, I woke.
Or maybe it was the thunderclaps and lightning
of another summer storm over the valley that shook
me back to this world. Curled against her sleeping
form, I felt our six-month child lightly kick
in rhythm to the flashing light, as if to speak
before the words had come. The small bones forming
in their rightful place soon calmed my nerves and broke
the lingering terror of the dream. Then I heard a crying
on the wind, not sad, not lost, but a kind of calling
between the worlds, a voice that I can remember hearing
as a child when I would lie in the tall grass and think
of ... what? What did thought consist of then but listening?

I move from bed to balcony to watch the lightning.
The air is electric, rich with riverscent. Another fork
shatters the black horizon, then a long pause, then another.
It's so beautiful, the quick light, brother to the low keening
of the storm, beautiful because it reveals to us that we're
cribbed in its bars, that our hearts will always be breaking
until we return to the darkness from which our life is born.

Child to Poet's Child
(June 1998)

Do you dream of the feel of grass?
My life will be my one true voice.
Do you hear the river running out?
I am all sea. I am full of sound.
Do you know the beat of your heart?
I know the song of the coming world.
When you meet an old man, an old woman ...
Yes?
Tell in your time that I love them.

IV

Love Letters

"Thank you for your letter of this morning. I was waiting for
the postman on the quay, looking unconcerned and smoking
my pipe. I love that postman! I've left orders in the kitchen
that he's to have a glass of wine to refresh him." – Flaubert to
Louise Colet

They come to us like little continents,
floes broken off the great Pangaea, when
we wish for them the speed of feathers
in the mouth of the running fox.

How the world and history wait on them!
Their white the apple-flesh in Adam's hand.
Did any vampire ever fall to a maiden's throat
with greater lust than lovers to an envelope?

Flaubert filled his with misery and Art –
"When I see a naked woman I imagine her skeleton."
And Sir Wilfrid Laurier was lawyer-clever
writing to his best friend's wife in conundrums.

Old-fashioned now, and gone the way of porches,
they arrive like flakes chipped off the Parthenon.
Soon, it will take a sanskrit skill to read their art.
Adieu and a thousand kisses to the francing of the heart!

were blue. He wrote a novel for them,
and several poems, but they filled up
with angry tears regardless
as the marriage soured, and no one
has looked into them now for eighty-seven years.

Hardy? He lived on and on in love with his melancholy,
her eyes becoming bluer and bluer, their beauty
alive, poignant, wild – the spoils of the heart
so often go to literature. Emma Lavinia Gifford,
skilled rider, Muse, snob, vicar's pious daughter:
no one thrills now to her gaze of vivid colour,
gone yellow on the pages of her husband's art.

Thus,
that I love a blue-eyed woman
is not the world's affair.
But listen, such a blue,
you have never seen the like ...

Eighty-seven years peer over my shoulder.

Walking to a Game of Pick-Up Football
One Autumn Afternoon,
I See an Adulterer
Rendezvous with His Mistress

The mist makes a low tackle on the Dutch elms
arrayed along both sides of the quiet side-street.
The leaves under her car tires and under my step
are crumpled notes he's written a hundred times
to his wife, without ever getting the words right.
His mistress is not young but lovely and parallel-
parks her sports car oblivious to my figure going by
just on the other side of his idling family van.
Indignant morality! I glide like a tall vowel
through the love-letters of a French woman, George
Sand perhaps, or Colette; I am young enough still
to be bold capital and pure apostrophe. O heart
coached in the stratagems of flesh. O red lips
parted and closing, moth-wings caught in flame.
As in a game played by teenagers in the fifties,
she moves from one car to another, and he drives
off with a sad intensity for the immediate future.
The mist rises, a lover who has stolen away
from the bed of the moon. Two blocks farther on,
three cars run a yellow caution light, like tacklers
enraged by the heart of the quarterback – what nerve
to beat in the middle of such chaos! The black gates
of the elms slam shut as I pass. O youth, how tiered
is the grave of your judgement, how unlovely the vowel
that cannot form the sound of loss.

College Town

Tall lilacs and long driveways. The moon
touches its chauffeur's gloves to every car-handle,
but no one wants to go for a drive. They are moored
in mahogany harbours, their bodies are the bone china
registered for the wedding of good taste and silence.
I am unshaven and uncouth as John Garfield before
the prettiest of the pretty Lane sisters, and I feel
I should have arrived to poison the Dean's daughter
against him and his world. I haven't, alas. I'm only
passing through until the next train ropes its black length
around my neck and hauls me out. But there are days, yes,
there are days when I could whisper social-democratic thoughts
into the seashell ears of debutantes, and smudge their tennis
whites with blue-collar caresses. Oh yes, and I could take the
Dean's cheque to get out of town, and leave ten pillows of tears
in my wake. You don't know what complacency does to the blood
of a man whose only books are paperbacks and used. Shove over
Moon, there's a good chap, I'm driving to the Sundance Pub;
you're welcome to join me, and the scent of the lilacs,
on the condition that you bring your pale daughters.

Je Veux's Just Another Phrase for
"Something that I'd Choose"

I want to write the longest line of poetry in our language
but I can't. I want to type Poe's "To Helen" into the auto-
matic teller and receive five thousand dollars in small
American bills while the line behind me grows longer than
the line of poetry I want to make the longest in our language
but can't. Sometimes I wish there were a "no-items" lane
at the grocery store so I could just walk past the cashiers
and say "hello" to their "hi," and "fine" to their "how are you?"
Do you have any idea how sad I am when the postman comes
and there's no letter for me, oh oh oh Mr. Postman, do you?
On days like this I wish a concert pianist would sit down
at the baby grand of my shadow and play all my mournful music,
the smudged, blurred notes of my past. I could promise him
or her an audience of cumulous posing as mink stoles on wealthy
dowager patrons, or perhaps a bag of macaroons from the store
if I could make my way past the line at the express checkout
which is longer than the longest line of poetry in our language
but I can't. I don't know what a fugue is, but I suspect
my life is currently experiencing one. There are dobermans
chained to all the gateposts of my childhood; I wish I could
say to them, "Fellas, I love those Nicean barks of yours,"
but I can't. Smile more often at strangers, my mother writes
in the meticulous and Elizabethanly black penmanship
for which she received excellent marks at Alexander Muir
Elementary School in downtown Toronto, Ontario, circa 1934.

If I were unhappy at the end of a century with fewer lines
and had my mother's beautiful flower-weighted hand, I'd write
the longest line of poetry in our lovely, lovely language,
I would
oh yes
I would.

The Apartment on Saskatchewan Drive

She left her glasses on the kitchen table in the sun-
light and lay down for a nap in another room while I
read poems, silently, on our fourth-floor balcony.
No one in the street below was shouting what I mouthed.
Not a single laughing child dreamed a common Russian grave.
Behind the sky, the stars were bunching like iced grapes;
below, a new current was changing the flow of the river.
My heartbeats were gentle and regular, doffings
of an old man's cap, slow veronicas for the cape of the sun.
I thought of nothing, as the streetlights pinged suddenly on,
but how quickly it happened, and how the definition of quickly
gave a rhythm to everything I loved, the summer night, her self
sleeping, words on a page, in a mouth, her self waking, dawn.
And then I turned and saw the very last of the sunlight shining
through the kitchen window onto her glasses.

Sweet time, our manifest dream, separation of body and spirit,
knowledge of the light that enters even as we're blind to it,
knowledge of the ripening heart on the sill of the world.

I waited for the first star, white as an apple's flesh,
then walked in and placed the sight of it softly on her lips.

On a City Avenue

The cotton summer dresses blow loosely on the rack
on the empty sidewalk outside the dress-shop.

They move only slightly, as if to cello music
being played overseas in another century.

Morning, and already warm. I know how the bee
feels slipping from the ripe flesh of the pear,

dazed, dripping, and eager for home. I hope
the salesgirls aren't watching from the store.

You were naked and sleeping when I left.
How is it, now, these dresses take your form?

I need a beatcop to cry out "move along there!"
a stronger breeze to be desire's chaperone.

Absence is only the idea of a presence
so powerful we never know what is here

and what is gone. The cotton summer dresses
blow loosely on the rack. They promise

to be filled and held and shivered down.
Is it any wonder that my face is warm?

Absent or present, my body thrills to your kisses.

v

Morenz

The crowds, the cheers, the broken leg, the death.
The crowds, the tears, the open casket, the death.
The standings, the headlines, the copy-mad press.
The rushes, the goals, the sainthood in Quebec.

Ontario boy, la première étoile, Habitant captain.
O Canada in the Forum, O Canada in the Gardens.
The dekes, the grace, the wrists, the soft hands.
The masses, the headlines, the hearse, the fans.

Six Team League. The Roaring Twenties. Hat Trick.
The Stanley Cup, the records, the move, the check.
The break, the cast, the fever, the held breath.
The death, the death, the death, the death.

The NHL

for Peter Cocking

Back when the boards were a chalky white
and we folded cards in the spokes of our bikes
and men named Gump patrolled the pipes

we tore our tennis-ball slapshots through
the fish-twine from nets my father had used
too many seasons in the Fraser's sloughs.

Back when hair-length defined who was who
when Eagleson and his cronies had started to screw
the players out of their union dues

our passes sluiced through the rain all night
those winters in the liquid streetlamp light
when we had to pretend to be on the ice.

Back when the Habs were French and flew
and their only jersey was bleu, blanc et rouge
and Disney's ducks were Donald and Scrooge

we sloshed down the wings in our rubber boots
and aimed waterlogged wrist-shots into the roof
like sophomore jinxes with something to prove.

Back when a blockbuster trade raised eyes
and goalies were peppered with cannonading drives
and Russians were lucky to escape with their lives

we squelched and swished for hours on end
moving to the Shakespeare of Gallivan
as if to a push from a godly hand.

The past is flawed except between friends –
Pete, we can go back whenever it rains
and scrub those rink-boards white again!

The Reel

I

A week of intense
heat after heavy rains. Milk chocolate still melts
in the sloughs and ditches, children on mowed lawns lie
on their shadows to peer at the pavement's mirages.
Dogs' tongues hang like pulled toffee. My
mother has given me a quarter for the matinee –
I gape from the shade and velvet plush, the butter
as golden on my fingers as the leopards born free
in their simmering savanna, as the leap of sun
I stumble back from, blinking. Across the street,
a man shakes hands vigorously with a garden-hose,
and in the sky a huge marshmallow browns in the heat.
I fade into the Daisy Dell for a cold Grape Crush.
My little breath is a genie gone back to the bottle.
All the way home, I drag behind me a sticky puddle.

In the backyard, my father holds a soggy pulp
of headlines and type; it is limp as a dead goose.
"Hi Monk, how was the show?" he asks, peeping
out from behind one wing. "There was leopards and
it was in Africa and some bad men wanted to shoot
the leopards with tyrannalizers," I answer, keeping
to the main plot. My father just winks and salutes
(he was in the Navy once) and returns to his goose.
His white t-shirt is like the moon with big craters.
I'm thirsty again, thirstier! So I go in the house

Acknowledgments

Some of these poems first appeared in the following magazines:

Canadian Forum
Event
Grain
Malahat Review
Matrix
Queen's Quarterly

"Final Night in Fort Chipewyan" and "Late August at the Mouth of the Fraser River" first appeared in *The Wilderness Anthology* (Outlaw Editions).

"Galiano Island, a Few Days Before Christmas" first appeared in a chapbook published by above/ground press.

"The Rhododendron" won first prize in the 1998 Orillia International Poetry Festival Contest.

My gratitude to Joan Harcourt at McGill-Queen's University Press, and to David O'Meara, Theresa Shea, and Russell Thornton for their encouragement and close readings of the poems. Also, thanks to Peter Cocking and Connie Reynolds for their help in finding a cover image.

Finally, I wish to acknowledge the financial assistance of the Canada Council and the Alberta Foundation for the Arts.

where my big sister languishes in her long hair
and scowls, just like the doused witch
in the movie where everybody follows the road
made of bricks like pats of hard butter.
The mummy of the fridge stands in the corner.
I'm almost twenty cents less than my mother's quarter,
too young to be anything but a bore to my sister.
But I don't care. I'm moving in movie-African weather.
Bwana! There's the fridge! Leap! Leopard! Leoparder!

II

Temple taps and Chaplin shuffles off the clapboard
screen of our neighbours' house and through the quiet
of licorice-black Ladner with only one streetlamp on
our street spilling melted butter. Grandma Atkey smiles
behind the big reel she'd taken out of its metal cover
and pretends that the moon is really her projector.
We gape from the dark and emerald plush of the lawn,
then follow pretty Shirley and funny Charlie home
the long way past the open door of the Chinese grocer's
where exotic harsh voices clash over games of mah-jongg.
Inside, someone makes a move and all the stars come out.
Silent and slow, we cross the earth like its credits.

III

The black and rolling never-ending film
of the Fraser River
better than a Cecil B. Demille epic
about the Roman Empire.
How long did I gape from the wet
and salty plush of the marsh,
all those salmon wrapped in crinkly tinfoil
deliciously out of reach,
and fishermen grubby as the Little Tramp
leaning on their oars
like canes?

No one can tell me that the years
aren't friends we only love the more
because they're missed.
I left the edit of thirty haircuts
on the cutting-room floor
of Mr. Holloway's barbershop
where they forever curl
in obsolescence like scenes
removed from a masterpiece
by Orson Welles. No matter.
We have it in us always to gape
at our lives from the plush rows
while the moon double-features the river.

Galiano Island, a Few Days Before Christmas

The old darkness of the world is on us again,
smelling of woodsmoke. Somewhere close by,
the ocean confesses its sin of coveting the shore
as it kisses the black robes of the firs.

The pub is twenty yards behind us, but already gone.
Our lodging is two miles distant. There is no moon,
no light, not even a Spanish vein in the throat
of the arbutus. We take each other's arms.

The stillness, the stillness. Is it God?
Someone is speaking who has no need of fire.
Is it Death? Someone is touching our bones.
Or is it just the love of the night for itself?

We move like geishas down the narrow road.
Burnt cedar. Soft-step of deer in the salal.
Faint rhythm of an orca's heart in the Pass.
A cold wind in the high boughs.

Final Night in Fort Chipewyan

On frozen Athabasca Lake
I stood alone, several hundred strides
from shore. February. Twilight. Somewhere
my name was written down in books, in files,
on old letters, called up on screens. Somewhere
a woman spoke my name to a friend, and smiled.
What happens when even the dogs fall silent
north of everything you've ever known?
Suddenly, it was as though the universe
had slipped beneath the ice, and my heart
sent a faint signal to my life on earth.
If someone had called my name just then,
I would not have turned. I was a new language
given substance by the kindness of the wind.
The moon rose slowly, detached from the snow.
I returned to my long sentence and my story,
found the low stars of the town, and headed in.

Cemetery at Olds
(en route to the Rockies for the weekend)

Late, we missed the highway turnoff to earth's more obvious beauty,
dragging the last light with us in a winding-sheet of dusk, to come upon
this lesser range, low peaks quarried from our mortal loss –
how long? a hundred years? Slowing, we shouldered close
enough to feel the utter blackness of the tombs, the weight
of the lowbranched windbreak-forest pressing down to buff the names –
no room for any but evergreen mourners, no room
for even the wind to wreathe the headboards of all sleep.

Three friends, and young, we'd driven half-a-mile past
the proper roadmap mark, to learn that all anarchic laughter
ends in awe of endings. Soon the night was shovelled
silent on our hood and roof. And flakes of snow began
to fall, as if in counterpoint to darkness, or
like missing dots that seek to join their dominoes
slow-toppling in this foothill calm, leaning, but never touching,
pushed by something ancient, starlight or grief, a long game
under the hard wood, played without us, but because of us,
because we hew remembrance from and for the ache of life.

Suddenly, but together,
shivering for the brevity of touch,
we burned our bones like so much paper
in the ashen air between the stones.

A Former Fisherman Enters a Used Bookstore at Night

He repeats his on-deck, blood-slick, squall-escaping motion
from the ocean's teem and wrack into a dim-lit cabin
only when
in lieu of dying fish and kerosene
and hours blowing heat on cold-cracked hands
he staggers out of darkness into book-crammed dens
where coughing browsers chart folded horizons.

Here is all the old rain of the world, caught
and dried and never to pelt the flesh or start
a shivering deep in the bones again – and yet,
there is always something of a storm in thought,
a chill wind on the page, stars, blood slopped
out of gills under boots, or someone's heart
adrift naked in the current, free of the net.

No one has to die to know the truth of death
or has to love to intuit love's blessedness.
Still, experience of experience only whets
the hunger for the blood of all that was,
and sends us back to weathers we know so well the dangers of.

So when he looses the fleet salmon of his shadow at the door
and carries the old scars in his palms across the creaking floor
to the mast-high shelves teetering with winds and stars
and the silence of marshes asleep in the moon, and hours
asking without speech for the sun, when he thinks of the years
he angled out of the raging dark into calm, thinks of the terror
and the after-fear, living and memory, youth and getting older,
and takes down a novel of another life, he simply stares
at the pages and would turn them forever,
trembling to see the face beyond the woman's bared shoulder.

Edwardian Street

A boarder coughs in an attic room,
a child's fever breaks, dark branches gull
the glass of an upstairs window, and someone
reaches for the Seneca on the shelf.

Old houses.

Something is happening at the end of their long hallways:
the heart of the past is foreclosing on itself.

Walking to Calm a Crying Newborn

for Dashiell

A street of houses, 2 am. The stillness of boxcars
at the edge of a continent.

Only the sun with its old gloves and union card
can unload what is here. Dreams, lives ...
but not even the sun knows the difference.

It is the infancy of winter. My breath chalks
the starlessness and the wind erases
what my breathing scribbled there.
Thirty years ago I could not read
the printed word, and now I find
I cannot read the thin smoke of the heart.

The moon is a tuft of sheep's wool snagged
on a briar. Or maybe it is the lost breath
of my childhood I'm meant to shepherd home.
I hold out the crook of my arm, and pull,
but nothing made of memory ever comes.

When will he know this truth, the child
I carry on my chest to soothe his crying?
His bones are as light as the snowflakes
that have just started falling; he breathes
not even strong enough to mark the board.

One day he will hold out his arm to find again
the friction and the script of his heart
but it will have burned off, like mine,
to be coal-ashes in the grates of houses
sitting still as boxcars.

But let him do this, for if the sun fails
to understand whether it wakes these sleepers
in their beds or puts them waking back to sleep,
it does not reject the task. Our lives
go always in the footsteps of old snowfalls
and lead always to the same silences.

Were our own hearts once so light and small?
A little frost is on his lashes, and one eye
has made a glass bottle for one tear.
I see it in the streetlamp's glow, and then
it breaks, soundlessly.

Nothing is as delicate as snowfall,
each flake the fingertip of a blind man
tracing the contours of a much-loved face.
I would that language were this way,
and love.

Simply,
my son gives back the warmth I give to him.
This truth about us I am not afraid to tell.

But the difference between solitude and loneliness?
How can we be certain the one is not the other?

Suddenly, despite the snow,
the night and street are darker,
except where, in one high window as we pass,

a candle slowly removes her wedding dress.

A Short Story Illustrating the Fate of the Poet's Work

A twelve year old boy dumps a bundle
of his local weekly paper in the tall grass
at the junction of a dead-end street
and the river. It's Wednesday afternoon,
threatening rain. He's late for baseball
practice, and so he pedals into the wild
green and tips the bundle from his
wire paper-basket; it lands with
a whump, but the blades soon settle
over the top front page photo
of a sunset behind the fishboats
in the harbour, never to be seen
by twenty-five faithful readers.

Just think of all they'll miss!
A sale on sirloin at the Shop-Easy,
how Council passed a new lawn-watering
bylaw, and how Mrs. Lillian English, eighty-four,
died in her sleep at the Westshore Laylum
Nursing Home, predeceased by her loving
husband of fifty-three years, Arthur English, Q.C.,
survived by one daughter, Edith, of Saskatchewan.

And then the sun goes down on the sun going down
and a beetle snuggles up to the black type
of the syndicated gardening column, and maybe one
or two readers have phoned to complain
that they didn't get their horoscopes or the flyers

with the coupons, and the boy, deliciously tired
from turning double-plays all afternoon
under the massing clouds, fades to sleep oblivious
of tomorrow's trouble, the crossed arms and scowl
of the circulation manager. And probably most
of the other good citizens whose doorsteps and porches
did not offer up the lacrosse scores or a few
careful quotes from the visiting MP, in town
for the Annual Oddfellows Salmon Barbeque,
have heard about the discounted beef and water
restrictions and poor old Mrs. English, though
it's true she reached a nice age, a shame her daughter
moved away and hardly ever visited.

And the nights and the years and the million
blossoms of the surrounding sour cherry, ten thousand
threats of storms carried out, wind
and rain and snow, washing over
the one week, fading the one sunset,
whatever mattered enough to be a headline
and what only made page three, and little
difference between them in the end,
the rescued cat, the expropriated land,
all the buying, selling, dying
that the earth took to its chest
and pulped, soft raft for the ladybug,
a paper accordion slowly, slowly pressed
and letting out a sigh that is the sigh
of all enduring, the twenty-five readers
and the loss that can't be reported
over the phone, that no one listens to,

the boy startled into middle-age, his hands
suddenly recalling the weight of the world and
the wonderful, freeing absence of it,
the buoyant ride away from the ended
into the still-to-be, while the little
black army of words in the grass
goes on fighting the red ants forever.